C000270358

THE   INFUSED SPIRITS

secrets

ANDREA STEVE MURPHY

THE INFUSED SPIRITS Secrets

by ANDREA STEVE MURPHY

© COPYRIGHT 2021 ALL RIGHTS RESERVED

This document is geared towards providing exact and reliable information with regard to the topic and issue covered. The publication is sold with the idea that the publisher is not required to render accounting, officially permitted or otherwise qualified services. If advice is necessary, legal or professional, a practiced individual in the profession should be ordered. From a Declaration of Principles which was accepted and approved equally by a Committee of the American Bar Association and a Committee of Publishers and Associations. In no way is it legal to reproduce, duplicate, or transmit any part of this document in either electronic means or in printed format. Recording of this publication is strictly prohibited, and any storage of this document is not allowed unless with written permission from the publisher. All rights reserved.The information provided herein is stated to be truthful and consistent, in that any liability, in terms of inattention or otherwise, by any usage or abuse of any policies, processes, or directions contained within is the solitary and utter responsibility of the recipient reader. Under no circumstances will any legal responsibility or blame be held against the publisher for any reparation, damages, or monetary loss due to the information herein, either directly or indirectly. The presentation of the information is without a contract or any type of guarantee assurance. The trademarks that are used are without any consent, and the publication of the trademark is without permission or backing by the trademark owner. All trademark and brands within this book are for clarifying purposes only and are owned by the owners themselves, not affiliated with this document.

PART TWO

INTRODUCTION

Infusion is an easy method of making a wide variety of liqueurs. Many of the world's most famous liqueurs are made using this method. Like Angostura bitters, which are also an infusion, there are often closely guarded formulas behind liqueurs, involving an amazing array of herbs and spices.

In spite of the secrecy, though, liqueurs can be easily made in your home distillery. Don't be intimidated by long lists of ingredients; if you've been making bitters or gin using these actual "botanicals" rather than flavorings, you already have a good start.

Liqueurs are simple beasts typically composed of three primary components: base alcohol, flavoring, and sweetener. Mix up those ingredients to your own cacophonous content and you may be rewarded with a bespoke bottle of deliciousness.

You can do this with very little equipment. At a minimum you should have some measuring cups, a small kitchen scale and an alcohol hydrometer for measuring the alcohol by volume (ABV).

Infusions are made by soaking, or infusing, various ingredients in base liquor, often vodka. Infusion times can be anywhere from a couple of days to many weeks. Generally the herbs and spices are infused, and then strained out of the liquid. By definition, liqueurs are sweetened; usually this is done after the botanicals have been infused.

Liqueurs may be sweetened with sugar, sugar syrup, honey or even agave syrup. Here are some recipes for popular liqueurs to get you started.

VODKA

1. Spicy Garlic-Habanero Vodka

Ingredients

- 1 medium garlic bulb

- 1 habanero pepper

- 1 (750-milliliter) bottle vodka

a) Separate the garlic into cloves and remove the skins.

b) Rinse the habanero pepper to remove any unwanted chemicals. Use the pepper whole or cut it in half, removing all seeds and most of the white flesh.

c) Place the garlic and habanero pepper into a clean quart-sized Mason jar.

d) Fill the jar with vodka. Secure the lid on the jar and shake well.

e) Store the infusion in a cool, dark place for 3 to 5 hours. Taste it after 3 hours, then every 1/2 hour after that until you get the desired flavor.

f) Strain the vodka through a fine-mesh strainer, coffee filter, or cheesecloth and into a separate container. Store as you would any other vodka.

g) Use in your favorite drinks, and enjoy.

2. Lavender-Rosemary Infused Vodka

Ingredients

- 1 (750-milliliter) bottle premium vodka

- 1 sprig fresh rosemary

- 2 sprigs fresh lavender

- Steps to Make It

- Gather the ingredients.

Rinse the herbs and place them into a clean quart-sized Mason jar or similar jar with a tight sealing lid.

Pour the vodka over the herbs and seal the lid tightly.

Shake a few times and store the jar in a cool, dark place for three to five days. Starting on the second day, test the flavor of the infusion daily.

Once the herbal flavor has reached your desired taste, strain the herbs from the vodka using a fine strainer or coffee filter.

Bottle and store as you would any other vodka. Use in your favorite cocktails and enjoy.

3.   Raspberry liqueur

- 1-2 lbs. of the best raspberries you can pick or buy
- 1 cup white sugar
- 1 bottle vodka or high-proof alcohol
- 1 sterilized quart canning jar or other glass jar with an airtight lid

a) Boil the canning jar or wash it well, rinse it in warm water, and pour boiling water into it. When the jar has cooled, pour out the water and put in the raspberries. Pour in the sugar and as much vodka as the rest of the jar will hold, leaving an inch or two clearance. Fit the jar with a sterilized canning lid and ring, or some other tight-fitting lid, depending on the jar.

b) Sometimes I put a barrier of plastic wrap between the jar and lid if I am not using a canning jar lid.

c) Put the jar in a dark place, but somewhere where you will see it every other day or so, perhaps near the coffee or tea. Shake the jar every day, or at least a few times a week for a month.

d) The sugar will dissolve gradually, and the color of the liquid will become a lovely red, while the raspberries will turn pale and uninteresting.

e) After the raspberries are almost white, let the jar settle, and carefully pour out the liquid. Some books say the fruit is now wonderful on ice cream, but I find it repulsive and throw it away.

f) NOTE: You can use this recipe for any berry or cherries. Every year I make pie cherry liqueur. Pit the sour cherries, add them to the vodka, and tie the pits in a bit of cheesecloth and add them as well. Some people crack a few of the pits for that almond flavor.

g) Also note that, especially with strawberries, you might get some globs of pectin floating around in the finished product. They are harmless but look disgusting. Filter them out when they form. I've never tried it, but it might be interesting to see if mashing the strawberries and adding half a teaspoon of pectic enzyme for twelve hours before adding the sugar and alcohol would help.

h) Taste the liqueur. If you want it sweeter, boil another $\frac{1}{2}$ to 1 cup of sugar with half the amount of water, cool it, and add in increments, tasting as you go. You will find that this procedure makes you quite cheerful.

i) I now filter the liqueur through a paper coffee filter, probably losing some alcohol content as I go, but that's life. You can also use several thicknesses of clean cheesecloth.

j) Store the liqueur in another jar or pretty bottle that has been cleaned and rinsed out with boiling water. Make sure the lid is tight. Keep in the dark to maintain the color.

4. Orange liqueur

- 1 pint dried orange and tangerine peels
- 1 cup sugar
- 1 bottle vodka
- 1 quart jar

a) Boil the canning jar or wash it well, rinse it in warm water, and pour boiling water into it. When the jar has cooled, pour out the water and put in the orange peels. Pour in the sugar and as much vodka as the rest of the jar will hold, leaving an inch or two clearance. Fit the jar with a sterilized canning lid and ring, or some other tight-fitting lid, depending on the jar.

b) Sometimes I put a barrier of plastic wrap between the jar and the lid if I am not using a canning jar lid.

c) Put the jar in a dark place, but somewhere where you will see it every other day or so. Shake the jar every day, or at least a few times a week for a month.

d) The sugar will dissolve gradually, and the color of the liquid will become a pale orange. It will take several months to leach the flavor out of the peels. Taste it once in a while to see how it's doing. There is likely to be a very firm layer of pectin on the bottom of the jar. Ignore it.

e) Let the jar settle, and carefully pour out the liquid.

f) Taste the liqueur. If you want it sweeter, boil another $\frac{1}{2}$ to 1 cup of sugar with half the amount of water, cool it, and add in increments, tasting as you go.

g) Filter the liqueur through a paper coffee filter or use several thicknesses of clean cheesecloth.

h) Store the liqueur in another jar or pretty bottle that has been cleaned and rinsed out with boiling water. Make sure the lid is tight. Keep in the dark to maintain the color.

i) This liqueur is infinitely useful. I make this with Everclear and use it for orange flavoring in cookies and cakes.

5. Watermelon Vodka

Ingredients

- 1 (750-milliliter) bottle vodka

- 1 small watermelon, cubed

- Steps to Make It

- Gather the ingredients.

In a clean, quart-sized infusion jar with a tight seal, place the cubed watermelon.

Pour the vodka over the fruit and shake a few times.

Seal the lid and store the jar in a cool, dark place for 4 to 6 days. Shake it once or twice a day. Beginning on the third day, test the flavor of the infusion daily.

Once the watermelon flavor is to your taste, strain the watermelon from the vodka. You may need to strain twice or use a cheesecloth to remove all of the fruit and seeds.

Wash the jar and return the flavored vodka to it. Store as you would any other vodka.

Mix the watermelon vodka into cocktails and enjoy.

6. Nut liqueur

- 2 lbs. fresh, unsalted, unblanched almonds, chopped OR the same amount of filberts or hazelnuts (though be sure they are fresh!)
- 1 cup sugar
- 1 bottle vodka or brandy
- 1 half-gallon jar or 2 quart jars

a) Rinse the jar out with boiling water.
b) Put the chopped nuts in the jar, and add the sugar and the vodka or brandy. Shake daily for a month or more until fragrant, then strain off the nuts, and add sugar syrup if desired. The color will be brown or tan. Filter or stand to clear. Nuts have oil in them, and so this will, too—it won't keep as long as fruit will, but it is quite nice to have around. Don't invite any squirrels over.

7. Banana Liqueur

- 2 medium-sized ripe bananas

- 3 cups vodka

- 1 teaspoon pure vanilla extract

- 1 cup sugar

- 1 cup water

Peel and mash the bananas. Combine banana, vodka, and vanilla extract in a jar; mix well. Cover tightly and let steep in a cool, dark place for 1 week. When steeping period is complete, strain and filter the liquid.

Combine sugar and water in a heavy saucepan. Bring to boil over medium heat. Reduce heat and simmer until sugar has completely dissolved, about 3 minutes. Remove from heat and let cool to room temperature.

Combine sugar syrup, mave, and the filtered liquid. Pour into bottles and cap tighly. Let age at least 1 month before serving.

8. Anisette(Licorice Liqueur)

- 2 tablespoons crushed star anise

- 3 cups vodka

- 2 cups sugar

- 1 cup water

Combine crushed star anise and vodka in a jar. Cover tightly and let steep in a cool, dark place for 2 weeks. When steeping period is complete, strain and filter the liquid.

Combine sugar and water in a heavy saucepan. Bring to a boil over medium heat. Resuce haeat and simmer until sugare has completely dissolved, about 3 minutes. Remove from heat and let cool to room temperature.

Combine sugare syrup and filtered vodka mixture. Pour into bottles and cap tightly. Let age at least one month before serving.

9. Plum Liqueur

- 1 pound fresh, purple plums (Santa Rosa preferred)

- 2 cups vodka

- 1 cup sugar

- 1 1-inch cinnamon stick cup water

- 4 whole cloves

Pit plums and cut plums into 1-inch chunks. Combine plums, sugar, cinnamon sticks, cloves and vodka in a large jar. Mix well. Cover tightly and let steep in a cool, dark place for 2 months. Shake jar occasionally.

When steeping period is complete, strain and filter the liquid.

Pour into bottles and cap tightly. Let age at least 1 month before serving.

10. Tangerine Liqueur

- 6 Tangerines

- 2 cups vodka or brandy

- $\frac{1}{2}$ cup sugar

- $\frac{3}{4}$ cup water

Using a swivel blade peeler, peel tangerines, scraping off peel only, avoiding the white membrane. Place peels in a jar with the vodka or brandy. Cover tightly and let steep in a cool, dark place for 3 weeks. Shake jar occasionally.

When steeping period is complete, strain and filter the liquid.

Combine sugar and water in a heavy saucepan. Bring to a boil over medium heat. Reduce heat and simmer until sugar has completely dissolved, about 3 minutes. Remove from heat and let cool to room temperature.

Combine sugar syrup with the filtered liquid. Pour into bottles and cap tightly. Let age at least 1 month.

11. Allspice Liqueur

- 3/4 tsp. allspice [presumably ground]

- 1 1/2 cups vodka or brandy

- 1/2 cup sugar syrup

Steep allspice in alcohol for 10 days. Strain and filter. Add syrup. Mature for 1-6 months.

12. Lavender Liqueur

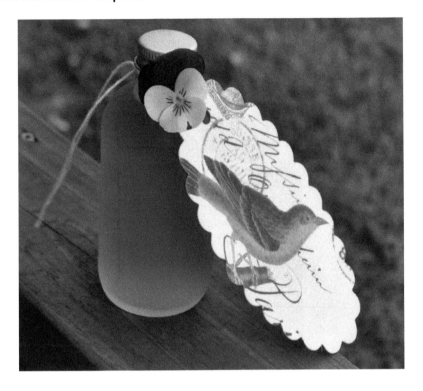

- 6 Tbsp Dried Lavender Petals

- 1 Fifth 80-Proof Vodka

- 1 Cup Sugar Syrup

a) Steep the petals inthe vodka for one week. Filter through cheesecloth and squeeze the petals to extract as much liquid as possible.

b) Add the sugar syrup and enjoy.

13. Green Tea Liqueur

- 6 tsp. green tea leaves (loose, good quality)

- 3 c. vodka

- 1 c. syrup

- 2-3 drops green food colouring

The tea leaves should be steeped in the vodka for only 24 hours; longer makes the liqueur bitter. Shake the jar or bottle well when you add the leaves. Add the sweetener and colouring the next day.

14. Cinnamon liqueur

Ingredient

- 1 Cinnamon stick

- Cloves

- 1 teaspoon Ground coriander seed

- 1 cup Vodka

- ½ cup Brandy

- ½ cup Sugar syrup (see recipe)

Steep all herbs in alcohol for 2 weeks. Strain and filter until clear and add sugar syrup to taste. Let stand 1 week and its ready to serve. Makes a nice hot drink when added to boiling water.

15. Vanilla-coffee liqueur

Ingredient

- 1½ cupBrown sugar; packed

- 1 cup Granulated sugar

- 2 cupsWater

- ½ cup Instant coffee powder

- 3 cupsVodka

- ½   Vanilla bean; split (or 2 teaspoons vanilla extract)

Combine sugars and water. Boil for 5 minutes. Gradually stir in coffee.

Cool. Add vodka and vanilla and mix thoroughly. Cover and let ripen for 1 month. Remove vanilla bean.

16. Fresh mint liqueur

Ingredient

- 1¼ cupFresh mint leaves, slightly packed *

- 3 cupsVodka

- 2 cupsGranulated sugar

- 1 cup Water

- 1 teaspoon   Glycerin

- 8 drops   Green food coloring (opt)

- 2 drops   Blue food coloring (opt)

Wash leaves in cold water several times. Shake or pat dry gently. Snip each leaf in half or thirds. Discard stems. measure cut mint leaves, packing lightly.

Combine mint leaves and vodka in aging container. Cap and let stand in a cool place for 2 weeks, shaking occasionally.

After initial aging, strain leaves from liqueur; discard leaves.

In a saucepan, combine sugar and water. Bring to a boil, stirring constantly. Let cool. Add cooled syrup to liqueur base, stirring to combine. Add glycerin and food color; pour into aging container for secondary aging of 1-3 more months.

A real good aging container is $\frac{1}{2}$ gallon canning jars. If you want more of this get the book " Classic Liqueurs;

The Art of Making and Cooking with Liqueurs " by Cheryl Long and Heather Kibbey.

17. Fresh orange liqueur

Ingredient

- 3 cups Vodka

- 3 Whole sweet oranges, cut into wedges

- ½ Lemon

- 2 Whole cloves

- 1 cup Basic sugar syrup*

Prep time: 15 mins Cook time: 0 mins Difficulty: **
Source: Gourmet Gifts By Dona Z. Meilach *To make
basic sugar syrup, combine 1 cup sugar with ½ cup water
in a saucepan. Bring to a boil over high heat and stir until

all the sugar is dissolved and the mixture is clear. Cool before using. Makes 1 cup.

In a wide - mouth jar, pour the vodka over the oranges, lemon and cloves so that the vodka completely covers the fruit. Seal tightly and let sit in a cool, dark place for 10 days. Strain through a paper coffee filter and discard the solids. Add sugar syrup. With a funnel, pour the liqueur into gift bottles and close tightly with corks or screw - on caps. Let sit for 3 to 4 weeks before using.

18. Strawberries with limoncello

Ingredient

- 30   Fresh strawberries cut into halves

- 4 teaspoons Limoncello liqueur; (20ml)

- Freshly ground pepper; sprinkled after

- ; taste

- 4 teaspoons Freshly squeezed orangg juice; (20ml)

Cut strawberries and put in a big bowl.

Add the orange juice, the liqueur and freshly ground prpper. Leave to marinate for at least 30 minutes.

Serve as it is, if wanted with Italian biscuits.

19. Fruit compote pie

Ingredient

- 1   9" pie crust

- 1 cup Dried apricots, chopped

- 1 cup Dried peaches and/or apples,

- Chopped

- 6 ounces   Apricot or peach nectar

- $\frac{1}{4}$ cup Peach or apricot liqueur

- 2 tablespoons   Dried cranberries, cherries

- Or raisins

- 1 cup Sour cream
- 1   Egg
- ⅓ cup Sugar
- 2 tablespoons   Flour
- ½ teaspoon Grated lemon peel
- pinch Nutmeg
- ½ cup Flour
- ⅓ cup Brown sugar, firmly packed
- ½ teaspoon Cinnamon
- ¼ cup Unsalted butter, melted
- ¼ cup Pecans or walnuts, chopped

Prepare pie crust and crimp. chill at least 15 minutes.

Bring apricots, peaches, nectar and liqueur to a boil; reduce heat and simmer 10 minutes. Stir in cranberries and continue to cook until fruit is soft and liquid is absorbed. Remove from heat and let stand while preparing rest of pie.

Preheat oven to 425F.

Sour Cream Batter:

Combine all ingredients until well blended; blend with filling and spoon into pie shell.

Crumb Topping:

Combine and scatter in an even layer on top of the filling.

Bake pie 15 minutes; reduce heat to 350F. and continue baking 20 to 25 minutes until crumbs are golden brown and filling is almost set.

Serve at room temperature.

20. Fruit-nut balls with liqueur

Ingredient

- 1 cup Chopped dates

- 1½ cup Seedless raisins

- ½ cup Dried apricots

- 1 cup Black walnuts -- chopped

- 2 cups Graham cracker crumbs

- ½ cup Southern Comfort

- ⅓ cup Honey

- 1 teaspoon   Orange peel -- grated

- 1 dash Salt

- 1 cup   Dried coconut

1. Put fruit, nuts and graham cracker crumbs through food processor or food chopper using the finest blade.

2. Mix together the honey, liqueur, orange peel and salt; add to fruit mixture. Mix well with hands and shape into marble-sized balls. Roll in the coconut.

3. Store in tightly covered container. Need not be refrigerated but store in a container with a tight-fitting lid.

21. Hot buttered cider

Ingredient

- 1 quart   Apple cider, preferably

- Freshly pressed

- $\frac{1}{4}$ cup Light corn syrup

- 2 tablespoons   Unsalted butter

- 2   Cinnamon sticks

- 3   Whole cloves

- 2 slices   Lemon

- 6 ounces   Apple liqueur

In a large saucepan, combine the cider, corn syrup, butter, cinnamon sticks, cloves and lemon slices.

Heat over a moderately low flame until the cider is hot and the butter is melted. Remove from the heat.

While the cider is heating, pour one ounce of liqueur into each of 6 mugs or heatproof glasses. Pour the hot cider into the mugs and serve at once.

22. Instant raspberry cordial jam

Ingredient

- 12 ounces   Raspberry jam

- 1 tablespoon To 2 Chambord or other

- Raspberry liqueur

Stir liqueur into jam; cover and refrigerate at least one day to allow flavors to meld.

23. Peppermint schnapps liqueur

Ingredient

- ⅓ cup Granulated sugar

- 1   Bottle; (16 oz) Light corn syrup

- 2 cups80 proof vodka

- 2 teaspoons Peppermint extract

1. Combine sugar and corn syrup in a 2 quart pan over medium heat. Heat until sugar dissolve, stirring regularly (about 5 minutes) 2. When sugar has dissolved, add vodka and stir well. Remove mixture from heat and cover

tightly with lid. Let cool. 3. Add peppermint extract to mixture and pour into a sealable bottle.

Makes 4 cups.

24. Lime liqueur

Ingredient

- 2   Dozen limes

- $\frac{1}{2}$ teaspoon   Ground cinnamon

- 6   Cloves

- 2 pounds   White sugar

- 6 cups 80 proof vodka

- 2 cups Water

- Green food dye

Wash limes. Slice each lime into 5 or 6 slices. Combine with cinnamon, cloves, vodka, water, and white sugar. Shake well until sugar is dissolved. Cover. Set in cool place for two weeks. Strain through fine sieve and leave alone to clear. Decant, pouring clear liquid into bottles. Tint a very very pale green color.

25. Liqueur & orange stuffing

Ingredient

- 18 ounces Package stuffing mix

- $\frac{3}{4}$ cup Butter

- 1 large Onion, finely chopped

- 1 cup Celery, minced

- $\frac{1}{2}$ cup Raisins

- $\frac{1}{2}$ cup Mandarin Orange Sections, chopped

- $\frac{1}{4}$ cup Sabra or Grand Marnier Orange Liqueur

- $\frac{3}{4}$ cup Hot water

- 1 Egg, beaten

(This recipe is for a 10-12 lb bird. Increase measurements for larger size.) Heat butter to foam. Add onion and celery, stirring in butter until wilted. Remove from heat and stir in stuffing, mixing along with the raisins, chopped orange sections, liqueur, hot water and egg. Spoon loosely into the bird's chest cavity.

26. Spicy herbal liqueur

Ingredient

- 6   Cardamom pods*

- 3 teaspoons Anise seeds*

- $2\frac{1}{4}$ teaspoon Chopped angelica root*

- 1   Cinnamon stick

- 1   Clove

- $\frac{1}{4}$ teaspoon   Mace

- 1   Fifth of vodka

- 1 cup   Sugar syrup (see recipe)

- Container: 1/2 gallon jar

Remove seeds from cardomom pods. Add the anise seeds, and crush all the kernals with the back of a fork. Put them in a 1-quart container adding angelica root, cinnamon stick, clove, mace, and vodka. Shake mixture well and store in a cupboard for 1 week. Pour through cheesecloth lined strainer several times. Blend the liquid with the sugar syrup. Ready to serve. *Most of these ingredients can be found at health food stores. This liqueur is similiar to Italian Strega and the spicy taste may not appeal to everyone.

27. Pineapple grand marnier

Ingredient

- 1 large   Glass container with a lid

- 1   Sweet pineapple peeled; cored and sliced

- 1   Bottle vodka; 750 ml

- $2\frac{1}{2}$ ounce   Pineapple infused vodka

- $\frac{3}{4}$ ounce   Grand Marnier

- Orange peel

To infuse the vodka. Place an entire ripe pineapple, peeled, cored, and sliced, in a glass container and cover with a bottle of vodka. Refrigerate pineapple for at least 48 hours.

To assemble the drink. Pour $2\frac{1}{2}$ ounces of pineapple infused vodka and $\frac{3}{4}$ ounces of Grand Marnier in cocktail shaker filled with ice.

Shake vigorously and strain into a chilled martini glass.

Garnish with orange peel.

28. Raspberry infused vodka martini

Ingredient

- 1.00   Twenty-five oz bottle vodka

- 1.00 pint   Raspberries; plus some for

- Garnish

- 6.00 ounce   Cointreau

Pour 1 bottle of vodka into a jar and add 1 pint of fresh raspberries. Let stand for 3 days Into a martini shaker, add 2 ounces raspberryinfused vodka, $\frac{1}{2}$ ounce Cointreau and ice. Shake, then strain into martini glass. Garnish with raspberries.

29. Papaya liqueur

Ingredient

- 1 Papaya

- 1 cup Vodka

- 1 small Lemon wedge, scraped peel

- $\frac{1}{4}$ cup Sugar syrup, optional to taste (see recipe)

Look for medium-sized papaya (slightly larger than a pear) with smooth, unbruised skin, and a fruity aroma. Best time is May and June. Dark spots on the skin are a bad sign and will cause a bad flavor (check stem for decay and softness). Cut papaya in half, remove seeds, and peel skin. Cut in medium chunks and place in vodka with lemon peel(twist to release flavor). Let steep for 1 week.

Strain and squeeze fruit, extracting juice. If desired, add sugar syrup. Store for 3 weeks

30. Blueberry liqueur

Ingredient

- 3 cupsFresh blueberries or blackberries

- 1 eachClove

- ½ cup Sugar syrup (see recipe) to taste

- 2 cups Vodka

- 1 each Lemon vedge, scraped peel

Note: Blueberries can be bought in season(May to Sept). Avoid stained baskets and DO NOT rinse until ready to use. If freezing, do so BEFORE rinsing. Rinse with cold water. Rinse berries and lightly crush. Add vodka, lemon peel, and clove. Pour in DARK bottle and store for 3-4 months. Strain through dampened cheesecloth squeezing out as much juice as possible. Add sugar syrup to taste and store another 4 weeks. Liqueur will tend to be on the watery side. Try adding glycerine if a thicker consistency is desired. Good for baking.

31. Chocolate liqueur

Ingredient

- 2 teaspoons Pure chocolate extract

- $\frac{1}{2}$ teaspoon   Pure vanilla extract

- $1\frac{1}{2}$ cup Vodka

- $\frac{1}{2}$ cup Sugar syrup (see recipe)

- $\frac{1}{2}$ teaspoon   Fresh mint (optional)

- drop Peppermint extract(optional)

Mix all ingredients and let mature 2 weeks. The chocolate tends to settle on the bottom and may need to be stirred before serving.

Finished version will tend to be thin, but is still quite tasty and excellent for mixing in coffee or pouring over desserts. Add glycerine to thicken if desired. For chocolate mint, add $\frac{1}{2}$ teaspoon fresh mint and a few drops of peppermint extract. Let mature 2 additional weeks.

32. Coconut liqueur

Ingredient

- 2 cupsPackaged coconut

- 4   Coriander seeds

- $\frac{1}{4}$ teaspoon   Vanilla extract

- 3 cupsVodka

- $\frac{1}{2}$ cup Brandy

Add all ingredients together and steep for 3-4 weeks.
Turn jar every few days. The coconut tends to be porous
and absorbs the alcohol so be sure to thoroughly strain
and filter the mixture to yield the largest amount.

Natural coconut may also be used, but tends to be watery and requires more coconut.

33. Curacao liqueur

Ingredient

- 3 tablespoons Bitter orange peel

- Dozen valencia or navel

- Oranges

- 2⅔ cup 80 proof vodka

- 1⅓ cup Water

- 2 cups White sugar

- 12 Whole cloves

- 1 teaspoon   Ground cinnamon

- 2 teaspoons Whole corriander seeds

Peel oranges. Section and cut each section into halves.
Put into the mixing jar along with the bitter orange peel,
cloves, corriander and cinnamon. Add sugar, vodka, and
water. Shake vigorously until the sugar is dissolved.
Leave to infuse for 5 weeks. Strain and leave to clear.
Be patient because this takes longer than most liqueurs.
When clear, decant off clear liqueur and bottle.

34. Grapefruit liqueur

Ingredient

- 6 Medium or large grapefruit

- 3 cups 80 proof vodka

- 1 cup Water

- 2 tablespoons Whole corriander seed

- 1 teaspoon   Ground cinnamon

- 4 cups White sugar

Cut or scrape off zest, yellow part of rind. Then peel
grapefruit and discard pith or white part. Separate

grapefruit sections and cut each section into several pieces. Combine the rest of the ingredients.

Cover. Leave to infuse for several weeks. Strain and let the liqueur clear for a week to 10 days. Carefully pour off the clear liqueur. If desired, a small amount of yellow food dye may be added for a stronger yellow color.

35. Honey liqueur

Ingredient

- 2 cups Vodka or brandy

- ¾ pounds Honey

- 3 tablespoons Orange rind, or 1/2 the

- Peel of an orange

- 1 cup Water, warm but not boiling

- 1 Clove

- 2 Cinnamon sticks, 2 inches each

Peel the orange find in one long spiral if possible, particularly if you want an attractive presentation. Disolve the honey in the water and add to the vodka and spices in an attractive bottle with the orange peel.

Let stand, well corked shaking every few days. I like the flavor well developed, and do not usually strain it at all, but check it after 2 or 3 weeks, and if you don't want too strong an orange spice flavor, strain the peel and spices out and rebottle.

36. Tea liqueur

Ingredient

- 2 teaspoons Black tea leaves*

- 1½ cup Vodka

- ½ cup Sugar syrup (see recipe)

Steep the tea leaves in vodka for 24 hours - NOT longer as a bitter taste will occur. Strain and add sugar syrup. Age for 2 weeks. *Your favorite tea may be used for the flavor you desire and spices can be added as well.

37. Peppermint liqueur

Ingredient

- 2 teaspoons Peppermint extract(or 3 ts)

- 3 cups Vodka

- 1 cup Sugar syrup

Combine all ingredients and stir. Let stand for 2 weeks.
Use 3 teaspoons of extract for a stronger mint taste
and additional sugar syrup for a sweeter thicker liqueur.

38. Angelica liqueur

Ingredient

- 3 tablespoons   Dried chopped angelica root

- 1 tablespoon Chopped almonds

- 1   Allspice berry, cracked

- 1   1" piece cinnamon stick, broken

- 3   To 6 anise or fennel seeds, crushed

- ⅛ teaspoon Powdered coriander seed

- 1 tablespoon Chopped fresh marjoram leaves or 1 tsp. dried

- 1½ cup Vodka

- ½ cup Granulated sugar

- ¼ cup Water

- 1 drop Each yellow and green food color,(optional)

Combine all herbs, nuts and spices with vodka in a 1 quart or larger aging container. Cap tightly and shake daily for 2 weeks. Strain through a fine muslin cloth or coffee filter; discarding solids. Clean out aging container. Place liquid back in container.

Place sugar and water in saucepan and stir to combine over medium heat.** When sugar is completely dissolved, set aside and let cool. When cool combine with food coloring and add to liqueur liquid. Cap and allow to age and mellow in a cool, dark place for one month.

39. Blueberries with orange liqueur

Ingredient

- 1 cup Orange flavored liqueur

- 1 cup Water

- 1 cup Sugar

- 1½ pounds Fresh blueberries

- 20 Fresh lavender flower heads

Prepare jars, lids and boiling water bath. Combine the liqueur, water and sugar in a pan and cook over med-high heat, stirring frequently, until sugar is dissolved and mixture has come to boil. Remove from heat.

Pick over, wash and dry blueberries, then pack them in hot dry jars, placing 4 lavender flower heads in each jar. Leave $\frac{1}{2}$ inch headspace. Pour hot liquid into jars, just covering berries. Wipe rims with clean towel and attach lids securely.

Place jars in boiling water bath, and when water returns to full boil, process for 15 mins.

40. Seed liqueur

- 4 tablespoons anise or caraway seeds, bruised or half ground
- 1 cup sugar
- 1 bottle vodka or brandy
- 1 quart jar

a) Put the seeds into a clean jar that has been rinsed out with boiling water. Add the sugar and the vodka or brandy. Shake daily for a month or more until fragrant, then strain off the seeds, and add sugar syrup if desired. The color will be tan. Filter or stand to clear.

41. Apple liqueur

- 2-3 lbs. tart/sweet flavorful apples
- 1 cup sugar
- 1 bottle vodka or brandy
- 1 half-gallon jar

a) Wash and core the apples, but don't remove the peel. Chop them finely. Rinse out the jar with boiling water. Add the sugar and the brandy and fit the jar with a lid. Shake every day for one to two months. Sometimes the peel will give it a rosy tint.

b) Strain out the fruit, filter, and add sugar syrup to taste. This also might develop a pectin haze, so be sure to filter.

42. Apricot or peach liqueur

- 1-2 lbs. dead-ripe apricots or peaches
- 1 cup sugar
- 1 bottle brandy or vodka
- 1 half-gallon jar or 2 quart jars

a) Wash and pit the apricots. Rinse the jar out with boiling water, add the apricots or peaches, sugar, and alcohol. Cover and shake once a day or so for one to two months. Strain and filter, then sweeten to taste with sugar syrup. These fruits are also nice lightly spiced with whole spices. Some people like to add a couple of the cracked pits to the fruit during soaking.

43. Coffee vanilla liqueur

- 2 ozs. good instant coffee
- 2 cups sugar
- 4 ozs. really good vanilla (do not use imitation vanilla)
- 1-2 Madagascar or Tahitian vanilla beans (optional)
- 1 bottle brandy or vodka

a) Rinse the jar out with boiling water. Drain.
b) Heat the water, coffee, and the sugar to simmer. Remove from the heat and cool. If you are using the vanilla beans, chop them fine, losing none of the black inner seeds, and put them in the jar. Add the 4 ounces of vanilla. Pour in the coffee/sugar/water and stir. After two to three months, strain out the vanilla beans. Bottle. You might want to add more sugar.
c) A tablespoon or two of this in chocolate cookies, cake batter, or icing is a wonderful addition. It doesn't overwhelm the chocolate but instead gives it more depth.

d) You can pour some rum or brandy over the vanilla beans after you have removed them; you will get more flavor out of them if you let them stand for another few months.

44. Sugar-shine

- 6 gallons (23 L) unchlorinated or filtered water
- 14 pounds (6.4 kg) granulated white sugar
- 1 package Turbo yeast (enough for at least 6 gallons wash)

a) In a large stock pot or mashing pot (at least 4-gallon capacity), bring 2 gallons of water to a boil. Turn off heat, add the sugar and stir to dissolve. Put 3 gallons of cold water in a fermenting bucket (8 gallons or larger), then pour in the hot water and sugar mixture. Stir to combine. Check temperature; you are aiming for about 38°C/100°F. Add more warm or cold water until there is a total of 6.6 gallons liquid (25 liters). Check temperature again. If it is over 38°C/100°F, just put the fermenter lid on loosely and let it cool down a bit. Check the specific gravity and record this number.

b) Add the yeast and stir vigorously until the yeast and nutrients are dissolved. Put on the lid, add the airlock and let it ferment at room temperature.

c) Depending on conditions, fermentation times can vary, so remember to watch the airlock for bubbling. Once the bubbling slows down noticeably, start checking the specific gravity once a day.

d) Once fermentation is complete, check and records the specific gravity.

e) Transfer the wash to the still with a siphon, leaving behind as much yeast sediment as possible. Record the volume of wash in the still and estimated alcohol content.

f) Distill in a column still.

45. Wheat Vodka

- 6 gallons (23 L) filtered or unchlorinated water
- 1½ teaspoons (7.5 ml) gypsum
- 8½ pounds (3.9 kg) flaked wheat
- 2.2 pounds (1 kg) wheat malt, crushed
- 1 package whiskey yeast/enzyme combination
- Have two large (at least 8-gallon capacity) fermenting buckets on hand.

a) Pour all the water into a large stockpot; I use my stainless steel 10-gallon mashing pot for this. Heat the water to 71°C/160°F. Stir in the gypsum, and then add the flaked wheat. Stir until the grain begins to liquefy; it will look something like oatmeal. The temperature will drop when you add the grain, so check it again. If it is below 67°C/152°F, heat gently until the temperature is between 67°-68°C/152°-155°F. Be sure to stir while it is heating. If the temperature is above 68°C/155°F, stop and let it cool until it is 68°C/155°F.

b) Add the wheat malt, stirring to incorporate. Put the lid on the pot and let the mash rest for 60 minutes. Stir gently and check the temperature every 15 minutes or so; it should stay at 65°C/149°F or above. After 60 minutes, use the iodine test to check for starch conversion. If conversion isn't complete, replace the lid and let rest another 30 minutes.

c) Let the mash cool to 32°C/90°F. Take a sample of the clear liquid on top of the mash and test the specific gravity. Record this number; it should be about 1.060 to 1.065 (remember to correct for temperature). Transfer mash, with the grain, to a fermenting bucket. Pour the mash vigorously back and forth between the two buckets several times to aerate the mash. Add the yeast, put the lid and airlock on the fermenter, and let ferment in a warm place until fermentation is done.

d) Strain the grains from the mash using a large straining bag. (See chapter 8 for information on feeding the mashed grains to your poultry or other livestock.) Let the strained liquid stand for several hours or overnight to let the yeast sediment settle.

e) Siphon the wash to the still. Be sure to record the volume of liquid, specific gravity and estimated alcohol content of the wash. Distill at least 3 times, starting with a stripping run.

46. Aquavit

- 50 ounces (1.5 L) good-quality vodka
- 3 tablespoons (45 ml) caraway seed
- 2 tablespoons (30 ml) cumin seed
- 2 tablespoons (30 ml) dill seed
- 1 tablespoon (15 ml) fennel seed
- 1 tablespoon (15 ml) coriander seed
- 2 whole star anise

- 3 whole cloves
- Peel of $\frac{1}{2}$ organic lemon, cut in strips
- Peel of $\frac{1}{2}$ organic orange, cut in strips
- 1 ounce (30 ml) simple syrup (optional)

a) Preheat your oven to 204°C/400°F. Toast the seeds on a foil-lined cookie sheet for 6 to 8 minutes; stir 2 or 3 times while they are toasting. Remove from oven and let cool briefly. Crush seeds lightly in a mortar and pestle, then put them in a large infusion jar (a half-gallon Mason jar works well). Add the star anise, cloves, lemon and orange peel, then the vodka. Add a bit more vodka if needed to completely cover the other ingredients. Seal tightly with a lid and shake briefly.

b) Infuse at room temperature for not less than 2 weeks. Shake the jar every 2 days while infusing. Strain, first through a strainer, then through cheesecloth or a coffee filter. Add the simple syrup, if using, and bottle. Best stored in the freezer.

c) Making citron (lemon) vodka is easy and quick.

47. Citron Vodka

- 1 bottle (750 ml) filtered vodka
- $\frac{1}{4}$ cup (60 ml) dried organic lemon peel

a) Peel of 3 fresh organic lemons, cut in thin strips, with no pith

b) In a half-gallon Mason jar, pour vodka over lemon peel and fresh rind. Cover and let macerate for 2 days. Smell and taste and strain out lemon rind as soon as the flavor and aroma suit your taste. Perfect for making the quintessential Cosmopolitan

c) If you plan to use dried citrus peel frequently, I suggest buying it in quantity. I get organic lemon, lime and orange peel by the pound at very reasonable prices from Starwest Botanicals (see Resources). For small quantities, though, it can be more cost-effective to make your own. It also gives you the choice of different types of fruit, especially with oranges, which can have bitter or sweet peel.

d) It's always best to buy organic citrus fruits when you plan to use the peel. Preheat your oven to its lowest setting. Using a vegetable peeler or sharp paring knife, cut thin strips of peel. Try to avoid cutting into the white pith. Cut the strips into small pieces, about $\frac{1}{4}$" by $\frac{1}{2}$". It's more important that the pieces be fairly uniform in size, so don't worry about the size too much. Spread the pieces on a baking sheet in one layer. Put the sheet in the oven and bake until the peel has shrunk noticeably; if you see the edges of the pieces starting to brown, take the sheet out of the oven. Depending on the temperature in your oven, this can take anywhere from 5 minutes to 20 minutes or so. The peel will continue to dry once it's out of the oven, so put the baking sheet on a cooling rack and let it sit until the peel feels dry. It can be used right away or stored in an airtight jar.

e) Did you know that there actually isn't all that much difference between gin and vodka? The main thing that makes gin different is that, at one point in the distillation, a special basket containing juniper berries and various herbs and spices is placed in the still. As the spirit begins to vaporize, the steam rises up through the basket, infusing the spirit with the familiar juniper tang of gin. Without this extra step, gin would smell and taste pretty much like one more vodka.

TEQUILA

48. Lemongrass-Ginger Infused Tequila

Ingredients

- 2 stalks fresh lemongrass

- 1 large piece fresh ginger

- 1 (750-milliliter) bottle blanco tequila

a) Peel the outer leaves from the lemongrass stalks, cut off the ends, and chop the remaining grass into thin rounds.

b) Place the lemongrass and whole ginger in the bottom of a clean quart-sized jar with a tight sealing lid.

c) Pour the tequila over the herbs and shake a few times.

d) Seal the lid tight and store the jar in a cool, dark place for about 2 weeks. Test the flavor of the infusion every day, beginning on the fifth day.

e) Once the flavor is to taste, strain the lemongrass and ginger from the tequila.

f) Wash the jar and return the flavored tequila to it. Store as you would any other tequila.

g) Use the infused tequila in cocktails, and enjoy.

49. Tequila (Agave Spirit)

- 2 bottles (44 oz. each) organic blue agave syrup
- 2 gallons (7.6 L) warm water, filtered or unchlorinated
- 1 package whiskey yeast/enzyme combination

a) Put 1 gallon of warm water in a fermenting bucket. Add the agave syrup and stir to dissolve. Stir in the second gallon of water. Check and record the specific gravity; it should be around 1.065 to 1.070. Make sure the temperature of the wash is 29°-33°C/85°-92°F and add the yeast. Put the lid and airlock in place and ferment.

b) Transfer the wash to your still and do a stripping run. Then do a spirit run on the low wines, distilling until the accumulated hearts are about 55% ABV.

50. Margarita liqueur

Ingredient

- 1 Bottle silver tequila

- 1 Peel of orange; cut in continuous spiral

- 1 Peel of lime; cut in continuous spiral

- 6 ounces Cointreau

Share a shot of tequila with a friend while making this. Add citrus peel to tequila remaining in bottle, and then add the Cointreau to taste. Keep refrigerated and serve in sherry glasses. Remove citrus peel if liqueur starts to become bitter. It can be served straight or on the rocks with a twist of orange peel.

Take a bottle of this to the host of a dinner party instead of a bottle of wine.

CONCLUSION

Your new bespoke liqueur can be drunk now but will improve if you let it sit in the bottle for 2-3 months. The flavors will meld together, and the alcoholic edges will smooth out.

Making liqueurs is a lot of fun and there are worlds of possibility within them. Hopefully this eBook has empowered you with enough basic information to get started. And remember to share your creations with friends when the trials of isolation are over! Cheers!

PART TWO

RUM

- **Coffee Liqueur**

- 1 recipe cold-brewed coffee
- ½ cup (125 ml) water
- ½ cup (125 ml) dark brown sugar (packed)
- 1 cup (250 ml) dark rum
- ½ vanilla bean

- First make the cold-brewed coffee. Bring the water and brown sugar to a boil on high heat; lower heat to a simmer, stirring to dissolve the sugar. Remove from the heat and let cool to room temperature, about 30 minutes.
- Add the cooled syrup and rum to the jar with the coffee. Using a knife, split the vanilla bean in half lengthwise and scrape out the seeds, add both the seeds and pod to the coffee mixture and stir to combine. Put the lid back on the jar and let it sit

at room temperature in a cool, dark place for at least 2 weeks, shaking once a day. Remove vanilla bean.

- **Mexican coffee liqueur cookies**

Ingredient
- ½ cup butter
- ½ cup cream
- ⅔ cup maple syrup
- ½ cup Kahlua or other coffee lique
- 1 teaspoon vanilla
- 1 each egg
- 2 cups white unbleached flour
- 1 teaspoon baking soda
- ½ cup oats
- ½ cup nuts
- 1½ cup mint carob chips

h) Cream together butter, cream, maple syrup, coffee liqueur and vanilla.

i) Stir in egg. Add flour in three additions, making sure each addition is thoroughly mixed. Add baking soda and oats. By hand, stir in nuts and mint chips. Drop by teaspoonful on an unoiled cookie sheet.

j) Bake at 350 degrees 10-12 minutes. Cookies will be golden brown.

- **Banana coconut rum cream liqueur**

Ingredient
- 2 Ripe bananas; mashed (about one cup)
- 2 teaspoons Coconut extract
- 1½ cup Rum
- ½ cup Vodka
- ½ cup Sweetened condensed milk
- ½ cup Evaporated milk
- 1 cup Cream of coconut

Mash bananas and blend in blender with coconut extract, rum, and vodka. Add milks and blend at low speed for one minute. Add cream of coconut or coconut milk and pulse stir for one minute (use lowest speed on blender and turn on-off eight times.) Makes about four cups.

- **Spiced Rum**

e) 1 750-milliliter (26 oz.) bottle of aged rum (I suggest dark rum, although not really dark or "black" rums)
f) 1 whole nutmeg
g) 1 cinnamon stick, broken into pieces
h) 1 vanilla bean, split lengthwise
i) 2 whole cloves
j) 1 cardamom pod
k) 4 black peppercorns
l) Sorghum Syrup
m) 1 star anise
n) 3 allspice berries
o) 1 large navel orange

- Place the whole nutmeg in an old pillowcase or wrap loosely in a clean kitchen towel and give it a firm whack with a hammer or mallet. Put the nutmeg and all the other spices in a heavy-bottomed sauté pan. Lightly toast spices over medium-high heat until fragrant, about 2 minutes. Remove from the heat and set aside to cool. Transfer them to a blade grinder and pulse around three to four times.
- Using a peeler, zest the orange, taking care to avoid any white pith. Put the zest in a 1-quart Mason jar and add the rum and toasted spices. Put the lid on securely, shake to blend and let it sit for at least 24 hours.
- Strain the spiced rum, first through a strainer, then through cheesecloth or a coffee filter. Pour into a clean glass jar or bottle and label.

- **Hazelnut crepes with ice cream**

Ingredient
- ½ cup Whole hazelnuts
- ½ cup Milk
- ⅓ cup Brewed coffee, cooled
- ⅓ cup Frangelico and/or kahlua
- 1 teaspoon Vanilla
- ⅛ teaspoon Almond extract
- 3   Eggs
- 1 cup Flour
- 3 tablespoons Unsalted butter, melted and
- Cooled
- Oil for pan
- 1 pint Coffee ice cream
- Caramel coffee nut sauce*
- Mocha fudge sauce

To toast hazelnuts:

- Bake in a 300F. oven, shaking several times, until skins darken, loosen and crack, about 15 minutes. Cool slightly, transfer to a towel. Fold towel to encase, rub vigorously to loosen the skins.

- Remove and discard as much of the skin as possible.

- Transfer skins to blender or food processor. Pulse on/off until finely chopped.

Crepes:
- Combine milk, Frangelico, vanilla and almond extracts and eggs until blended. Add flour al at once and beat until smooth and all of the flour has been absorbed. Beat in the hazelnuts, butter and sugar.

- Cover and refrigerate at least two hours, but preferably overnight.

- Return batter to room temperature.

- Heat crepe pan until water spits across. Lightly oil and heat until hot. Remove pan from heat, pour in $\frac{1}{4}$ cup batter and swirl quickly to coat bottom. Return pan to heat.

- Cook until crepe is golden brown on bottom; turn and cook other side.

- Transfer to plate, separating crepes with waxed paper. Repeat with remaining batter, oiling pan as needed.

- The crepes can be prepared to this point ahead of time. Rewarm by removing waxed paper, wrapping in tin foil and baking in a preheated 350F. oven on a cookie sheet for about 15 minutes.

- Quickly roll warm crepes around small scoops of ice cream. Serve with one or both of the sauces.

- **No-bake mocha liqueur balls**

Ingredient
- 3 cups Vanilla wafer crumbs; about 250 g box
- ¼ cup Water
- 3 tablespoons   Instant coffee
- 4 ounces   Semisweet chocolate
- ½ cup Tia Maria
- 1½ cup Sifted powdered sugar
- Pecan halves; optional

Place water in a medium size saucepan. Add coffee and stir over low heat until coffee is dissolved. Add chocolate and continue heating just until melted, stirring frequently. Remove from the heat and stir in liqueur.

Blend wafer crumbs and sugar together; stir in liquid ingredients until well mixed. Shape into 1 inch balls. If desired, press a pecan piece in the center of each, flattening slightly. Store in a tightly covered container in a cool place for a least a week to allow flavors to blend. Makes about 3 dozen.

- **Jasmine tea liqueur**

Ingredient
- 1 pint Dark rum
- $\frac{1}{2}$ cup Jasmine tea
- 1 cup Sugar syrup

Steep the tea in the rum for 24 hours, and remove.

Make the sugar syrup by boiling 1 cup of sugar in $\frac{1}{2}$ cup of water (it will be VERY thick). When the syrup cools, add to the rum. It's ready to drink immediately. This is a very nice after dinner liqueur, but you may drink it any time you want to. If the tea flavor is too strong, try steeping for a shorter time, cutting down on the amount, etc. Likewise, the amount of sugar may be a bit excessive for many tastes, so experiment.

- **Mocha cream liqueur**

Ingredient
- 1 14 oz. can sweetened condensed milk
- 1 cup Dark rum
- 1 cup Heavy cream
- $\frac{1}{4}$ cup Chocolate - flavored syrup
- 4 teaspoons Instant espresso coffee powder
- $\frac{1}{2}$ teaspoon   Ground cinnamon
- $\frac{1}{2}$ teaspoon   Vanilla extract
- $\frac{1}{4}$ teaspoon   Coconut extract

Combine all the ingredients in a food processor or blender container.

Cover and process on high speed until the mixture is well blended and smooth. Serve the cordial at once over cracked ice or ice cubes. Or, transfer the mixture to a tightly - covered container and refrigerate for up to 2 weeks. Stir just before serving.

- **Swedish fruit in liqueur**

Ingredient
- 1 pint Blueberries
- 1 pint Raspberries
- 1 pint Strawberries
- 1 pint Red currants
- 1 cup (or more) granulated sugar
- ⅔ cup Brandy
- ⅔ cup Light rum unsweetened whipped cream for garnish

Remove stems and hulls from berries. Rinse, drain, and place in glass serving bowl. Add sugar, brandy, and rum, stirring with a wooden spoon. Taste and add more sugar, if needed. Marinate overnight in refrigerator. Serve with whipped cream and a generous amount of sauce. Serves 6 to 8.

- **Coconut-almond torte**

Ingredient
- 6 larges   Eggs,   separated,   at   room temperature
- 1 cup Sugar
- 1 cup Almonds, coarsely chopped
- 2 cupsUnsweetened shredded coconut
- $\frac{1}{2}$ cup Orange juice
- $\frac{1}{4}$ cup Sabra liqueur (or Grand Marnier or Cointreau)
- Oil for the pan
- Grated bitter chocolate for garnish
- Whipped cream for garnish

Preheat oven to 325 degrees. Lightly grease 10" spring form pan. In large bowl, beat egg whites to soft peaks; add $\frac{1}{2}$ c. of the sugar; beat to stiff peaks.

In another bowl, beat yolks with remaining $\frac{1}{2}$ c. sugar until light and fluffy. Add almonds and coconut; mix gently. Fold in the egg whites.

Pour batter into pan; bake 45 min. or until crust is light brown on top and toothpick comes out clean. Remove from oven and let sit in the pan a few minutes. Prick the top of the torte all over with a toothpick.

Combine orange juice and liqueur and pour over the torte while still in the pan. When torte is completely cool, remove and serve with whipped cream, if desired, and grated chocolate.

- **Coffee liqueur sauce**

Ingredient
d) 1 tablespoon   Coffee liqueur
e) $\frac{1}{4}$ cup   Lemon juice
f) $\frac{1}{4}$ cup   Onion, finely chopped
g) 6 dashes Hot pepper sauce
h) $\frac{1}{2}$ teaspoon Honey
i) $\frac{1}{8}$ teaspoon Ginger root, grated
j) $\frac{1}{4}$ cup   Lime juice
k) $\frac{1}{4}$ cup Vegetable oil
l) 1 teaspoon Worcestershire sauce
m) $\frac{1}{2}$ teaspoon Dill weed
n) $\frac{1}{4}$ teaspoon White pepper

Shake all ingredients together well in covered jar. Let stand 1 hour or longer to blend flavors. Shake well before using. Pour over fish and marinate 30 minutes. Grill fish, basting often..

- **Cranberry cordial**

Ingredient
- 8 cupsRaw cranberries, coarsley

- Chopped

- 6 cupsSugar

- 1 litre Light or amber rum

Place the chopped cranberries in a gallon jar with a tight fitting cover (or divide between to half-gallon jars). Add the sugar and the rum. Close the jar tightly; shake gently to blend. Store in a cool dark place for 6 weeks, stirring or shaking the contents every day.

Strain the cordial into decorative bottles. Seal with corks.

Note: This recipe can be halved or even quartered. For a half recipe, use 4 cups cranberries, 3 c sugar, and $2\frac{1}{2}$ cups rum; for a quarter recipe, use 2 cups cranberries, 1 $\frac{1}{2}$ cups sugar and 1 $\frac{1}{4}$ cups rum.

•Creamy rum liqueur

Ingredient

- 1 can (400-ml) condensed milk

- 300 milliliters Cream

- 300 milliliters Milk

- $\frac{3}{4}$ cup Rum

- 2 tablespoons   Chocolate sauce

- 2 teaspoons Instant coffee dissolved in

- 2 teaspoons Boiled water

Mix all ingredients slowly in a blender. Serve chilled. Keeps sealed in the fridge, for 2 weeks.

•Eagle brand irish cream liqueur

Ingredient

- $1\frac{1}{4}$ cupIrish Whiskey; or brandy, rum, rye whiskey, bourbon, scotch

- 14 ounces Sweetened condensed milk

- 1 cup Heavy cream

- 4 Eggs

- 2 tablespoons Chocolate flavored syrup

- 2 teaspoons Instant coffee

- 1 teaspoon Vanilla extract

- ½ teaspoon Almond extract

In blender container, combine all ingredients, blend until smooth.

Store tightly covered in refrigerator up to one month. Stir before serving

MALT WHISKEY

- **Upper Dungeness Bourbon**

- 2 ounces (60 ml) ginger liqueur
- 2 ounces (60 ml) bourbon
- ½ organic lemon

- Put the ginger liqueur and lemon in a cocktail shaker or mixing glass. Muddle well with muddler or a long wooden spoon. Add about one cup of cracked ice and the bourbon. Stir well until the glass is frosty. Pour into cocktail glass or wine glass; do not strain. Garnish with a lemon slice.
- Purists will insist a smash isn't a smash without mint, so go ahead and garnish with fresh mint if you like.

- **Bacon-Infused Old Fashioned**

FOR THE BOURBON- BACON INFUSION:

f) 3 or 4 slices bacon, or enough to render 1 ounce of fat (PDT uses Benton's, but any extra-smoky variety will do)

g) 1 750-ml. bottle of bourbon such as Four Roses Yellow Label

FOR THE OLD FASHIONED:

- 2 ounces bacon-infused bourbon

- 1/4 ounce Grade B maple syrup

- 2 dashes Angostura bitters

- Twist of orange

FOR THE BACON-INFUSED BOURBON: Cook bacon in pan and reserve rendered fat. (1) When bacon fat has cooled a bit, pour off one ounce from pan. (2) Pour bourbon into a non-porous container. (3) Strain the bacon fat into the container and infuse for 4 to 6 hours at room temperature. Place mixture in freezer until all the fat is solidified. With a slotted spoon, remove fat and strain mixture back into bottle.

FOR THE COCKTAIL: In mixing glass, stir 2 ounces bacon-infused bourbon, maple syrup, and bitters with ice. Strain into chilled rocks glass filled with ice. Garnish with orange twist.

- **Peach liqueur**

Ingredient

- 1½ pounds   Peaches; peeled & sliced*

- 1½ cup Sugar

- 4 Lemon peel; strips

- 3 Whole cloves

- 2 Cinnamon sticks

- 2 cups Bourbon

*Use fresh peaches for this recipe In medium glass bowl, thoroughly combine all ingredients. Heat 10 minutes on POWER LEVEL 7 (Medium-High) until sugar is dissolved, stirring once. Continue cooking on POWER LEVEL 1 (Warm) an additional 30 minutes, stirring twice. Cover and let stand 3 to 4 days. Strain before using.

•Chocolate creme liqueur

Ingredient

- 2 cupsHeavy cream

- 14 ounces Sweetened condensed milk

- 1 cup Whiskey

- $\frac{1}{4}$ cup Unsweetened cocoa powder

- $1\frac{1}{2}$ tablespoon Vanilla extract

- 1 tablespoon Instant espresso powder

- 1 tablespoon Coconut extract

In a food processor, combine cream, sweetened condensed milk, whiskey, cocoa, vanilla, espresso powder, and coconut extract. Process until well blended and smooth. 2. Serve immediately over ice. Or place in glass container, cover tightly, and store in refrigerator up to 3 weeks. Stir before using.

- **Scotch-style Malt Whiskey**

f) 5 gallons (19 L) filtered or unchlorinated water
g) Backset or citric or tartaric acid, as needed to adjust the mash water pH (see chapter 8)
h) 15 pounds (6.8 kg) malted two-row barley
i) ½ pound (225 g) peated malt
j) 1 package whiskey yeast with enzymes
k) 2 tablespoons (30 ml) plain yogurt or dried cheese making culture

- Ready to taste my first malt whiskey!
- Put 2½ gallons of the water in an 8- or 10-gallon stockpot and heat to 71°C/160°F. Stir in the malted barley and peated malt. Hold the temperature between 67°C/152°-155°F for 90

minutes. Use the iodine test to check for starch conversion. Strain the grains from the wort into an 8-gallon fermenting bucket, using a large straining bag. Leave the bag suspended in the fermenter. Heat 5 quarts of the remaining water to 74°C/165°F. Pour this water through the grains in the bag. Heat the remaining 5 quarts of water to 82°C/180°F and repeat the rinsing of the grains. Let the grains drain thoroughly into the fermenting bucket, then set the grains aside.

- Why Is It Called "Single Malt"?
- At first glance, I thought this simply meant that the whiskey was made with one kind of malt. Actually, single malt by definition means a 100% malt whiskey that has been produced at one distillery. It may be a blend of malt whiskies of different ages. If it contains whiskies from different years, though, the age statement on the bottle will refer to the youngest whiskey in the blend.
- Cool the wort to 33°C/92°F. Check the specific gravity and record. Add the yeast and yogurt or cheese culture. Ferment at room temperature for 2 to 6 days, or until fermentation has slowed considerably or stopped. Check the specific gravity again and record this number.
- Transfer the wort to your still, leaving the yeast sediment in the wort. Do a stripping run first; you should have low wines around 30% ABV. Then do spirits run, switching from heads to hearts when the emerging distillate reaches 80% ABV. Collect

hearts until the emerging distillate is down to 60% to 62% ABV before switching to tails.

- Save the heads and tails from all whiskey spirit runs and mix them together in a glass jar or bottle. Add a small amount of this mixture (called "feints") to your next whiskey spirit run. This is commonly done in commercial distilleries, and is part of the mystique; somehow the added feints improve the flavor of the finished whiskey. It works just as well in small batches like this.

- **"sinful cherry" liqueur**

Ingredient
- 2 One quart jars
- 2 slices Lemon
- 1 Fifth V.O.
- Bing cherries
- 2 tablespoons Sugar

Fill each jar half full with cherries. Add to each one slice lemon and one tablespoon sugar. Then fill to the top with V.O. Put the lid on tight, shake and put in cool place for 6 months. The cherries are the most delicious part of the drink; feed one to your lover!

- **Irish whiskey**

- 5 gallons (19 L) filtered or unchlorinated water
- 7½ pounds (3.4 kg) malted two-row barley, cracked
- 7½ pounds (3.4 kg) unmalted barley, cracked
- Backset or citric or tartaric acid, as needed to adjust the mash water pH (see chapter 8)
- 1 ounce (30 ml) distiller's yeast
- 2 tablespoons (30 ml) plain yogurt (optional)

b) Heat 2½ gallons of water to 71°C/160°F. Adjust pH if needed. Add cracked unmalted barley, then the malted barley and stir to moisten all the grain. Hold the mash temperature at 67°C/152°F for 90 minutes. Drain liquid from grains into fermenting bucket. Heat 5 quarts of water to 74°C/165°F and wash the mashed grains; drain the liquid into the fermenting bucket. Heat the remaining 5 quarts of water to 82°C/180°F and rinse the grains as before.

Pour all the liquid into the fermenting bucket and mix well.

c) Cool to about 29°C/85°F; check and record the specific gravity. Add the yeast and the yogurt (if using). Put the lid and airlock in place and ferment in a warm spot for 72 to 96 hours.

d) Transfer the wash to your still and do a stripping run. Your low wines should be around 30% ABV. Do a spirit run, making the heads cut when the emerging distillate reaches 80% ABV. Switch to tails when the emerging distillate is about 55% ABV. Now do one more spirit run on the hearts from the first spirit run. Distill this run as before, but only until the accumulated hearts are between 80% to 90% ABV.

- **Easy whiskey liqueur**

- 1 bottle whiskey
- 2 cups orange blossom honey
- zest of 2 oranges or tangerines
- 4 tablespoons coriander seeds, bruised

c) Rinse out the jar with boiling water. Drain.
d) Mix everything together in the jar, put the lid on, and shake once a day for a month. Taste, and decide if you want more honey or more orange flavor. Strain or filter, and bottle the liqueur.

- **Bourbon Recipe**

- 5 gallons (19 L) filtered or unchlorinated water
- 10 pounds (4.5 kg) cracked corn
- 1¼ pounds (0.6 kg) cracked rye berries
- 1¼ pounds (0.6 kg) flaked wheat
- 2½ pounds (1.1 kg) malted barley
- 1 package whiskey yeast/enzyme combination

c) Heat the water in a large stockpot to 71°C/160°F. Stir in the corn, rye berries and flaked wheat, followed by the malted barley. Put the lid on the pot and hold the temperature at 66°-68°C/152°-155°F for 60 minutes. Test for starch conversion using the iodine test, and hold for up to another 60 minutes if necessary for full starch conversion.

d) Cool the mash to 33°C/92°F. Transfer the mash to an 8-gallon fermentation bucket. Add yeast. Ferment hot (29°-32°C/85°-90°F if possible) for 2 to 4 days.

Strain the liquid from the grains. Check and record the specific gravity of the wash.

e) Transfer the wash to your still, including the yeast, and do a stripping run. The low wines should be about 30% ABV. Next do a spirit run, making the cut to hearts when the emerging distillate is down to 80% ABV. Distill until the accumulated hearts are between 68%–75% ABV.

f) Age your bourbon using heavily charred oak chips. I suggest 4 to 6 months for anything up to a gallon, maybe 2 to 3 months if you have less than half a gallon.

g) 20-kilo (44 pound) bags of organic cracked corn for making bourbon and other whiskies.

h) Variations on the Bourbon Theme

i) Rye adds spicy notes to whiskey. To ratchet up the spice in your bourbon (known as high rye bourbon), simply increase the proportion of rye in your formula. For wheated bourbon, try replacing the rye in the basic recipe with flaked wheat. Wheat can add smoothness to whiskey, but beware of adding too much; it might tone down the bourbon character more than you wanted.

- **Rye Whiskey Recipe**

- 5 gallons (19 L) filtered or unchlorinated water
- 10 pounds (4.5 kg) cracked rye berries
- 2½ pounds (1.1 kg) malted rye
- 2½ pounds (1.1 kg) cracked malted barley
- 1 package whiskey yeast/enzyme combination
- 2 tablespoons plain yogurt or dried cheese making culture (optional)

k) Heat the water in a large stockpot to 71°C/160°F. Stir in the rye berries and malted rye, followed by the malted barley. Put the lid on the pot and hold the temperature at 66°-68°C/152°-155°F for 60 minutes. Test for starch conversion using the iodine test, and hold for up to another 60 minutes if necessary for full starch conversion.

l) Cool the mash to 33°C/92°F. Transfer the mash to an 8-gallon fermentation bucket. Add yeast and yogurt or cheese culture (if using). Ferment at room temperature for 2 or 3 days. Strain the liquid from the grains. Check and record the specific gravity of the wash.

m) Transfer the wash to your still and do a stripping run. The low wines should be about 30% ABV. Next do a spirit run, making the cut to hearts when the emerging distillate is down to 80% ABV. Switch to tails when the emerging distillate is down to 62%–65% ABV.

GIN

- **Cajun martini**

Ingredient

- 1.00   Jalapeno pepper; sliced up to stem

- ½   Bottle Gin

- ½   Bottle Vermouth

- Pickled green tomato

Add jalapeno to gin bottle, fill gin bottle up to lip with vermouth.

Refrigerate 8 to 16 hours (but no longer). Strain through a double layer of cheesecloth in a funnel into a clean bottle. Pour into chilled glass. Garnish with pickled green tomato.

- **Roast boar with liqueur**

Ingredient

- 1 Leg of wild boar

- 1 tablespoon Juniper berries

- 1 tablespoon Coriander seeds

- 1 tablespoon Coarse sea salt

- 2 tablespoons   English grain mustard

- Snipped leaves of a good sprig of

- ; rosemary

- Grated zest of 2 lemons and juice of 1

- ; lemon

- 1 tablespoon Freshly-ground black pepper

- $\frac{1}{4}$ pint Gin

- 4 tablespoons Blackcurrant liqueur; (4 to 5)

- 2 pounds Celeriac; (2 to 3)

Have the skin removed from the boar in one piece, trim off most of the fat and wipe the meat all over.

Grind the juniper berries, coriander and rosemary with the salt and mix with the rest of the ingredients. Rub the paste over the meat, cover with the skin and leave for an hour or two, or overnight if more convenient.

Preheat the oven to 150C/300F/gas 3. Peel and trim the celeriac into cork-sized pieces and arrange in a greased roasting dish. Place the haunch on top, cover with the skin and put into the oven.

Cook for 25-30 minutes per pound, plus at the end of cooking, an extra 20 minutes at 200C/400F/gas 6. Allow the meat to stand for 20 minutes before carving into thin slices.

Serve with extra root vegetables roasted in the oven, or steamed vegetables such as celery, leeks and fennel. Make a gravy with the boiled down meat juices and serve with a little home-made sharp fruit jelly.

BRANDY

- **David's Orange Liqueur**

- About 32 ounces (1 L) brandy (homemade or at least not the cheapest stuff out there)
- 2 pounds (0.9 kg) organic mandarin oranges
- ½ cup (125 ml) dried organic sweet orange peel
- Simple syrup

g) Note: I highly recommend using organic citrus fruits any time you're using the peel; non-organic fruits may have pesticide residues that you don't want in your infusions, so it's easier to avoid these by choosing organic.

h) Have two clean 1-quart wide-mouth Mason jars ready. Peel the mandarin oranges and cut the peels into fairly small pieces; this increases the surface area of the peel that will be exposed to the brandy. Divide the peel between the two jars. Add half of the dried orange peel to each jar. Add brandy to each jar to within about an inch of the top. Put lids on. Let the jars sit at room temperature, away from the sun, for at least 2 days; I have let it go up to a week with good results. Shake the jars gently at least once a day. After the first 2 days, begin smelling the infusion every day and stop infusing when the aroma is agreeable to you.

i) Strain the fruit out of the brandy. You should have around 25 to 28 ounces (750 to 875 ml) of liquid. Add simple syrup to taste and bottle. As a guideline, we used 1 teaspoon (5 ml) simple syrup for each fluid ounce of liqueur; add a little at a time and taste until the sweetness suits you, and be sure to make a note of how much simple syrup you used! I suspect you will like this liqueur so much that you will be making it again.

j) The liqueur is ready to use, but I recommend letting it sit in a cool dark place for at least a month.

- **Amaretto liqueur**

Ingredient

b) 1 cup   Granulated sugar

c) $\frac{3}{4}$ cup   Water

d) 2 Dried apricot halves

e) 1 tablespoon   Almond extract

f) ½ cup   Pure grain alcohol and

g) ½ cup   Water

h) 1 cup   Brandy

i)   3 drops Yellow food coloring

j)   6 drops Red food coloring

k)   2 drops Blue food coloring

l)   ½ teaspoon   Glycerin

Combine sugar and ¾ cup water in a small saucepan. Bring to a boil, stirring constantly. Reduce heat and simmer until all sugar is dissolved. Remove from heat and cool.

In an aging container, combine apricot halves, almond extract, grain alcohol with ½ cup water, and brandy.

Stir in cooled sugar syrup mixture. Cap and let age for 2 days. Remove apricot halves. (Save apricot halves, as they may be used for cooking). Add food coloring and glycerin. Stir, recap and continue aging for 1 to 2 months.

Re-bottle as desired. Liqueur is ready to serve but will continue to improve with additional aging.

- **Chocolate mousse cake**

Ingredient
- ½ cup Granulated sugar
- ½ cup Water
- 8 tablespoons   (1 stick) unsalted butter
- 12 ounces   Semisweet or bittersweet chocolate
- ⅓ cup Sweet liqueur, such as Cointreau or Chambord
- 6 Eggs
- 1 cup Heavy cream
- 2 tablespoons   Sugar
- 1   Basket fresh raspberries (optional)

Preheat the oven to 325 degrees and set a rack in the middle level. Butter an 8-inch round pan and line the bottom with a disk of parchment or waxed paper cut to fit. Butter the paper. Cut the chocolate finely and set it aside.

Combine the sugar and water in a saucepan and bring to a boil over low heat, stirring occasionally to make sure all the sugar crystals dissolve.

Remove the syrup from the heat and stir in the butter and chocolate; allow to stand 5 minutes. Whisk smooth.

Whisk in liqueur and eggs, one at a time, into the chocolate mixture, being careful not to over mix.

Place 1 inch of warm water into a small roasting pan. Pour batter into the prepared 8-inch round pan and bake about 45 minutes, until set and slightly dry on the surface. Remove round pan from the roasting pan and cool to room temperature in the pan and cover with plastic wrap. Refrigerate dessert in pan. To unmold, run a knife between the dessert and the pan and pass the bottom of the pan over the heat. Invert and remove paper. Invert to a platter.

To finish, whip the cream with the sugar until it holds a soft peak. Spread the whipped cream on the top of the dessert. Decorate the top with the raspberries.

- **Apricot Liqueur**

- 1 cup water

- 1 pound dried, pitted apricots

- 1 tablespoon powdered sugar

- 1 cup sliced almonds

- 2 cups brandy

- 1 cup sugar

- 1 cup water

Place water in a saucepan, bring to boil and remove from heat. Add apricots and let soak for 10 minutes or until most of the water is absorbed. Let cool. Drain off any remaining water.

Place apricots in a jar and spinkle with powdered sugar. When sugar has dissolved, add almonds and brandy. Stir well to mix. Cover tightly and let steep in a cool, dark place for at least 2 weeks. When steeping period is complete, stain and filter liquid.

Combine sugar and water in a heavy saucepan. Bring to boil over medium heat. Reduce heat and simmer until sugar has completely dissolved, about 3 minutes. Remove from heat and let cool to room temperature.

Combine sugar syrup with the filtered brandy mixture. Pour into bottles and cap tightly. Let age at least 1 month before serving.

•Chocolate liqueur shells

Ingredient

- 3 ounces Each of semi-sweet or bittersweet, milk and white

- 3 ounces White chocolate, chopped

- 2 Eggs, separated

- 1 tablespoon Each of Tia Maria, crème de

- Chocolate, melted in separate bowls menthe or Cointreau

- food coloring if desired

With a spoon, smear melted chocolate evenly over inside of 12 paper cups. Turn cups upside down on a plate. Refrigerate until set. Gently peel off the paper.

Slowly melt white chocolate. Remove from heat; quickly beat in egg yolks. Set aside. In a separate bowl, beat egg whites until stiff, but not dry. Divide egg yolk min into three separate bowls and add 1 teaspoon of a different liqueur to each bowl. Add a drop or two of green food coloring to bowl containing creme de menthe - if desired.

A drop or two of yellow coloring can be added to Cointreau mixture. Gently fold a third of the egg whites into each of the bowls.

Spoon into chocolate shells. Refrigerate 2 hours. These shells should be consumed within 24 hours. The chocolate cases can be made ahead of time and stored in a cool, dry place.

- **Strawberry liqueur jam**

Ingredient

- 500 grams Strawberries

- 1 medium Green apple

- Juice of 1 lime

- $1\frac{3}{4}$ cup Sugar

- 2 tablespoons Grand Marnier

Wash & hull strawberries. Peel, core & finely chop apple. Add lime juice & let stand covered for 30 minutes. Microwave the fruit & juice for 4 minutes on high. Add sugar, stir & microwave 35 minutes on high, stirring

every 10 minutes. Stand five minutes, pour into warm
sterile jars. Seal.

- **Raspberry liqueur**

Ingredient
- 4.00 cup   Clean dry raspberries
- 4.00 cup   Brandy
- 2.00 cup   Sugar
- $\frac{1}{2}$ cup Water

Put the raspberries into a jar and cover with the brandy. Seal and store on sunny windowsill for 2 months. Put the sugar in a saucepan with the sugar and heat only enough to dissolve the sugar. Pour the syrup onto the raspberry liqueur. Strain and bottle.

- **Apple Liqueur**

- 1 pound red delicious or other sweet apples

- 1 2-ince cinnamon stick

- 2 whole cloves

- 2 cups brandy

- 1 cup sugar

- 1 cup water

Cut apples in quarters and remove cores, do not peel. Cut quarters in half.. Combine apples, cinnamon stick, cloves, and brandy in a large jar. Cover tightly and let steep in a cool, dark place for 2 weeks.

When steeping period is complete, stain and filter liquid. Combine sugar and water in a aheavy saucepan. Bring to a boil over medium heat. Resuce heat and simmer unitl sugar has completely dissolved, about 3 minutes. Remove from heat and let cool to room temperature.

Combine sugar syrup with the filered brandy mixture. Pour into bottles and cap tightly. Let age at least 1 month before serving.

- **California eggnog**

Ingredient
- 1 quart   Cold prepared eggnog
- 1½ cup Apricot brandy
- ¼ cup Triple Sec
- Nutmeg, for garnish

In a largepitcher, combine the eggnog, apricot brandy and Triple Sec.

Stir well to blend.

Cover and refrigerate at least four hours to blend flavors.

At serving time, garnish each serving with a sprinkling of nutmeg.

- **Chocolate liqueur sundaes**

Ingredient

- ¾ cup Braum's or Smucker's fatfree fudge topping

- 1 each (1.3oz) prepared Dream Whip

- 6 Tb Kahlua

- 6 Tb Cointreau

- 6 Tb Grape Nuts Cereal

- 1 quart Frozen nonfat vanilla yogurt or fat free ice cream

Spoon 2 tablespoons fudge topping into each of 6 brandy snifters.

Place a scoop of frozen yogurt in each; top with dream whip. Drizzle 1 tablespoon of each liqueur over each snifter. Sprinkle with Grape Nuts.

- **Fruit compote infused in tea**

Ingredient

- 3 Rounded tsp Earl Grey tea leaves; (3 to 4)

- 400 millilitres Boiling water; (14fl oz)

- 3 Strips lime zest; (3 to 4)

- 1 Lime; juice of

- 100 grams Caster sugar; (3 1/2oz)

- 3 tablespoons Cooking brandy; (3 to 4)

- 75 grams Dried peaches; (2 1/2oz)

- 75 grams Dried apricots; (2 1/2oz)

- 75 grams Dried cranberries; (2 1/2oz)

- 2 Fresh pears; peeled, cored and; sliced

- 2 Fresh ripe dessert appled; peeled, cored and; sliced

Infuse the tea leaves in 250ml (9fl oz) boiling water for 5 minutes, then strain. Discard the leaves. Put the strained tea infusion into a pan with the lime zest and sugar and simmer until the sugar has dissolved. Boil for a few minutes to reduce slightly and to slightly thicken the mixture. Add the brandy and lime juice. Arrange the dried and fresh fruits in a serving bowl and pour the syrup over. Leave for 3-4 hours before serving.

- **Cheesecake marble**

Ingredient
- 8½ ounce   Package chocolate wafers
- ⅜ cup Unsalted butter, melted
- 6 ounces   Bittersweet chocolate,
- Finely chopped
- ⅓ cup Coffee, freshly brewed
- 2 pounds   Cream cheese, softened
- 1 cup   Sugar
- 4 Eggs, at room temperature
- 1 cup Yogurt, plain
- 2 tablespoons   Grand Marnier or other
- Orange flavored liqueur
- 1 teaspoon   Vanilla
- ¼ cup Flour
- ¼ teaspoon   Salt

- 1 tablespoon Grated orange peel

Preheat oven to 325F. Butter side only of a 9 inch springform pan; wrap outside with tin foil and set aside.

Pulverize wafers in food processor. Combine crumbs with melted butter and press evenly over bottom and up sides of pan; set aside.

Melt chocolate in coffee; beat until smooth. set aside.

Beat cream cheese until creamy and smooth. Slowly beat in sugar until smooth and creamy. Beat in eggs, one at a time, until incorporated.

Beat in yogurt, Grand Marnier, and vanilla. Lower speed and beat in combined flour and salt.

Stir melted chocolate into $1\frac{1}{2}$ cups of the batter. Stir orange peel into plain batter.

Pour orange batter into prepared pan. Put chocolate batter, in 8 plops, on top. Swirl with table knife until marbled to your liking.

Push any crumbs that are higher than the batter onto it creating a crumb border.

Bake until firm around edge, but still wobbly in center, about an hour. Cool in pan on wire rack. Gently release side of pan. Serve at room temperature or chilled for a firmer consistency.

- **Cherry wishniak liqueur**

Ingredient
- ½ pounds   Bing cherries
- ½ pounds   Granulated sugar
- 2 cups Vodka or brandy

Wash and stem cherries and place them on a towel to dry. Gently put cherries into a 1-quart jar. Pour sugar over cherries. Do not stir or shake. Pour vodka or brandy over sugar and cherries. Do not stir. Cover tightly with a lid and put the jar on a high shelf in a dark cabinet. Let it stand for 3 months without stirring or shaking. Strain into a 1-quart bottle; the cherry meat will have dissolved. Yield 2-½ to 3 cups.

- **Almond Liqueur**

- 1 cups sugar

- 1 cup water

- 2 cups vodka

- 2 cups brandy

- 4 teaspoons almond extract

Combine sugar and water in a heavy saucepan. Bring to a boil over medium heat. Reduce heat and simmer until sugar has completely dissolved, aobut 3 minutes. Remove from heat and let cool to room temperature.

Combine sugar syrup, vodka, brandy, and almond extract. Pour into botttles and cap tightly. Let age at least 1 month before serving.

- **Pear Liqueur**

- 1 pound firm ripe pears

- 2 whole cloves

- 1 1-inch cinnamon stick

- Pinch of nutmeg

- 1 cup sugar

- 1cups brandy

Core pears and cut into 1-inch chunks, do not peel. Place in a jar with cloves, cinnamon, nutmet, sugar and brandy.

Cover tightly and let steep for 2 weeks at room temperature. Shake jar daily. When steeping period is complete, strain and filter the liquid.

- **Ginger Liqueur**

- 2 ounces (60 g) fresh ginger root, peeled
- 1 vanilla bean
- 1 cup (250 g) sugar (or ¾ cup (175 ml) honey)
- 1½ cups (375 ml) water
- Zest of 1 organic orange or ¼ cup (60 ml) dried organic orange peel
- 1½ cups (375 ml) brandy
- Again, I recommend using brandy as the base for this delicious liqueur. Slice the ginger thinly. Split the vanilla bean lengthwise.
- In a saucepan, bring the ginger, vanilla bean, sugar and water to a boil. Lower heat and simmer for 20 minutes. Remove from heat and let cool.

- Pour the syrup into a jar (don't strain it), add the orange zest or peel and the brandy. Seal, give it a shake, and let it steep for a day; remove the vanilla bean and let it steep at least one more day. I let mine steep for 5 days total with good results, but then I like a lot of ginger flavor.
- Strain into a bottle. Let it sit for at least 2 weeks (if you can stand it) before using.

COGNAC

- **Grand orange-cognac liqueur**

Ingredient

- ⅓ cup Orange zest

- ½ cup Granulated sugar

- 2 cupsCognac or French brandy

- ½ teaspoon Glycerin

Grand Marnier is a classic orange liqueur to be savored. While ordinary brandy can be used, we recommend a good cognac or French brandy for best flavor. Ready in 5 to 6 months. Makes about 1 pint.

Place zest and sugar in a small bowl. Mash and mix together with the back of a wooden spoon or a pestle.

Continue mashing until sugar is absorbed into the orange zest and is no longer distinct. Place into aging container. Add cognac. Stir, cap and let age in a cool dark place 2 to 3 months, shaking monthly.

After initial aging, pour through fine mesh strainer placed over medium bowl. Rinse out aging container.

Pour glycerin into aging container and place cloth bag inside strainer. Pour liqueur through cloth bag. Stir with a wooden spoon to combine. Cap and age 3 more months before serving.

- **Fresh figs curacao**

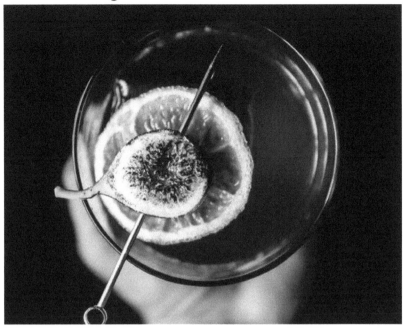

Ingredient

- 12.00 Fig, fresh; peeled & quartered

- 1.00 tablespoon Cognac

- 1.00 cup Heavy cream, whipped

- ⅓ cup Curacao

Marinate the figs in the cognac 30 minutes or longer. Mix the cream and Cura#ao. Fold in the figs and any cognac that they have not absorbed.

BITTERS

- **Orange Bitters**

- Zest of 3 organic oranges, cut into thin strips
- $\frac{1}{4}$ cup (60 ml) dried organic orange peel
- 4 whole cloves
- 8 green cardamom pods, cracked
- $\frac{1}{4}$ teaspoon (1 ml) coriander seeds
- $\frac{1}{2}$ teaspoon (2 ml) dried gentian root
- $\frac{1}{4}$ teaspoon (1 ml) whole allspice
- 2 cups (0.5 L) high-proof vodka (don't skimp on cheap brands here)
- 1 cup (250 ml) water
- 2 tablespoons (30 ml) Rich Syrup

- Put the orange zest, dried orange peel, spices and gentian root into a 1-quart Mason jar. Add the vodka, adding a bit more if needed to completely cover the ingredients. Put on the lid and store at room temperature for 2 weeks. Shake the jar gently once a day.

- Strain the liquid, using cheesecloth or a coffee filter, into a clean 1-quart Mason jar. Repeat straining until all sediment is removed. Squeeze the cheesecloth to force through as much liquid as possible. Transfer the solids to a small saucepan. Cover the jar and set aside.

- Pour the water over the solids in the saucepan and bring to a boil on medium heat. Cover the pan, reduce the heat to low and simmer for 10 minutes. Remove from heat and let cool completely.

- Add the liquid and solids in the saucepan to another 1-quart Mason jar. Cover and store at room temperature for a week, shaking the jar every day. Strain the solids out, using cheesecloth, and discard the solids. Add the liquid to the jar with the original vodka mixture. Add the rich syrup, stir to mix well, then put the lid on and shake to blend and dissolve the syrup.

- Store the jar at room temperature for 3 days. Then skim off anything that floats to the surface and strain it once more through cheesecloth. Use a funnel to bottle it, and you're done! These bitters have the best flavor if used within a year, although they will last almost indefinitely.

MIXERS

- **Homemade Tonic Water**

- 4 cups (1 L) water
- 1 cup (250 ml) chopped lemongrass (roughly one large stalk)
- $\frac{1}{4}$ cup (60 ml) powdered cinchona bark
- zest and juice of 1 orange
- zest and juice of 1 lemon
- zest and juice of 1 lime
- 1 teaspoon (5 ml) whole allspice berries
- $\frac{1}{4}$ cup (60 ml) citric acid
- $\frac{1}{4}$ tsp (1 ml) kosher salt

- Homemade syrups for making tonic water (left) and ginger ale.

j) Combine ingredients in a medium saucepan and bring to a boil over high heat. Once mixture starts to boil, reduce heat to low, cover and simmer for 20 minutes. Remove from heat and strain out solids using a strainer or chinois. You'll need to fine-strain the mixture, as it still contains quite a bit of the cinchona bark. You can use a coffee filter and wait for an hour or more, or do as I do and run the whole mixture through a French coffee press.

k) I've had very good results simply letting the mixture stand undisturbed for at least a few days, and up to a week. This works especially well in the refrigerator. The solids settle to the bottom, and you can either rack the clear liquid off or carefully pour it into another clean jar. It takes a bit longer this way, but I think it's worth it.

l) Once you're satisfied with the clarity of your mix, heat it back up on the stovetop or in the microwave, and then add $\frac{3}{4}$ cup of agave syrup to each cup of your hot mix. Stir until combined, and store in the attractive bottle of your choice.

- **Farms Ginger Syrup**

In a stainless steel or enamel stockpot, combine:

- 9 cups (2.04 kg) sugar (I use organic white sugar; brown sugar gives a different flavor)
- 18 cups (4.3 L) water, preferably unchlorinated or filtered
- 6 ounces (180 g) fresh organic ginger, thinly sliced (peeled or unpeeled, as you prefer)
- Cover and bring to a boil over medium-high heat, stirring to dissolve sugar. Once the syrup comes to a rolling boil, turn off heat. Leave the lid on and let steep for at least 10 minutes. While the syrup is heating, thinly peel and juice:

- 3 organic lemons (since you're using the peel, you really want to use organic lemons for this)

- Divide the lemon peel pieces into 6 even piles. Remove ginger pieces from syrup with a slotted spoon or small sieve. Strain the seeds from the lemon juice and add juice to the hot syrup.
- Taking the jars one at a time, empty out the water and put one pile of the lemon peel in the jar. Using a canning funnel, fill the jar with hot syrup to within $\frac{1}{4}$" of the top and seal with the canning lids and rings. Let cool completely on rack. Remove rings before storing. Label jars and store in a cool place. Refrigerate after opening.

- **Ginger Syrup a Jar at a Time**

To make ginger syrup one quart at a time, use the following quantities:

- 1½ cups (375 ml) sugar
- 3 cups (750 ml) water
- 1 ounce (30 g) fresh ginger
- Juice and peel of ½ organic lemon

h) For a stronger ginger taste, leave one slice of ginger in the jar before sealing the lid.
i) Besides the aforementioned Canadian whiskey and ginger ale, here are a few suggestions for using ginger syrup:

- **Just Plain Ginger Ale**

- 2 shots ginger syrup
- 5 to 6 ounces (150 to 180 ml) soda water

- You might also try drizzling ginger syrup over your fruit salad and yogurt in the morning. How about using the ginger syrup in a marinade for pork roast? Once you've tried it, I bet you'll come up with more ways to use this versatile syrup.

- Orgeat

51. 2 cups (500 ml) raw almonds, sliced or chopped

52. 1½ cups (375 ml) sugar

53. 1¼ cups (300 ml) water

54. 1 teaspoon (5 ml) orange flower water (or homemade orange bitters)

55. 1 ounce (30 ml) vodka

Mix

- **Maraschino liquor**

c) Maraschino Cherries
d) Fresh cherries (a sour variety is best), washed and pitted
e) Maraschino liqueur or brandy or bourbon

Loosely fill a clean 1-quart Mason jar with cherries. Add maraschino liqueur, brandy or bourbon to completely cover them. Put the lid on the jar and refrigerate. They will be ready to use in about a week. For best flavor, use within a month or so. (Trust me, once a jar of these is opened, you won't have any trouble using them up.)

- **Soda pop**

- 4 ozs. Homebrew brand extract, any flavor OR 4-6 ozs. other extracts (be sure to shake the bottle before using)
- 2½ gallons water
- 4½ cups sugar
- ¼-½ tsp. champagne yeast
- 24-28 12 oz. beer or soda bottles and crown caps

c) Dissolve the yeast in one cup of the water at body temperature, and let it sit for five minutes.

d) Mix the sugar and most of the extract with enough of the rest of the water to dissolve the sugar in the primary fermenter at warm body temperature (not over 100°).

e) They say to use warm tap water, but I've heard it isn't good for you to use warm or hot tap water for anything other than washing, so I would advocate using cold tap water, adding boiling water until you get the right temperature. Use your floating thermometer or apply the scientific guess-and-by-golly test of dipping your wrist in the water to see how hot is it...carefully. Dipping in your big toe is not acceptable.

f) Stir until you don't hear any of the sugar scraping along the sides and bottom and you are sure the sugar is dissolved. A clean metal spoon is fine for this purpose.

g) Now add the yeast and the rest of the warm water. Taste it and see how you like it. Add the last ounce or so of the extract. Sometimes the strength differs from package to package, so this is a way of making sure it isn't too strong. You can always add a little more water and sugar, too.

h) Fill the drained, rinsed bottles with your racking tube, leaving an inch or two in the neck. Seal with a crown capper. Make sure the seals are good.

i) Rinse off the outsides of the bottles, and put them in a covered cardboard box (a beer case is good). Keep them in a cool (but not cold), dark place for a couple of weeks. If you are nervous, place the box near a drain in case you mismeasured the sugar.

j) Before you serve, chill the bottles for at least an hour, and open them carefully over the sink. There will be a little sediment on the bottom, so once you start pouring, just keep going until you get to the sediment and stop. The sediment won't hurt you, but it isn't pretty. Serve your sparkling beverage with pride.

k) I tend to make a sugar syrup instead of going the dry sugar route, because I think the carbonation is more even.

l) If using honey, use a tiny bit more than you would sugar. Boil it into a syrup, especially if you are serving this to very young children, who should not eat uncooked honey.

m) Champagne bottles and a bench capper make this whole process go a lot faster.

n) There's no law saying you can't blend extracts!

o) I make my own ginger beer extract by simmering four to eight ounces of fresh sliced ginger for an hour or two. However, it's trickier to do because you can't always predict how much flavor any one stem of ginger will have. Still, sometimes it's fun to live a little dangerously, and Jamaican ginger beer spoiled me. If you try this, add the zest and juice of two to three lemons or 2 to 3 teaspoons citric acid to the brew.

p) NEVER add more sugar than is recommended in the instructions!!!

q) Soda pop made this way will keep for up to a year if it is kept cool, or about three months in warm weather.

CONCLUSION

Your new bespoke liqueur can be drunk now but will improve if you let it sit in the bottle for 2-3 months. The flavors will meld together, and the alcoholic edges will smooth out.

Making liqueurs is a lot of fun and there are worlds of possibility within them. Hopefully this eBook has empowered you with enough basic information to get started. And remember to share your creations with friends when the trials of isolation are over! Cheers!